ANIMAL
families

P9-DHA-988

DK Publishing

I love hide and seek.
Mommy will never
find me up here!

DK

LONDON, NEW YORK,
MELBOURNE, MUNICH, and DELHI

Written and edited by Lorrie Mack
Project Designer Gemma Fletcher

Designers Mary Sandberg, Sonia Moore
Editors Penny Arlon, Alexander Cox, Penny Smith
US Editor Margaret Parrish

Consultant Kim Dennis-Bryan PhD. FZS

Publishing Manager Bridget Giles
Managing Art Editor Rachael Foster
Category Publisher Mary Ling

Production Controller Claire Pearson
Production Editor Clare McLean
Jacket Editor Mariza O'Keefe

First published in the United States in 2008 by
DK Publishing
375 Hudson Street, New York, New York 10014

Copyright © 2008 Dorling Kindersley Limited

AD406-05/08

All rights reserved under International and Pan-American
Copyright Conventions. No part of this publication may be
reproduced, stored in a retrieval system, or transmitted
in any form or by any means, electronic, mechanical,
photocopying, recording, or otherwise, without the prior
written permission of the copyright owner. Published
in Great Britain by Dorling Kinderley Limited.

A catalog record for this book
is available from the Library of Congress

ISBN 978-0-7566-4224-2

Color reproduction by Alta Image, UK
Printed in Singapore by Star Standard Pte Ltd

Discover more at
www.dk.com

contents

Just like us	4—5
Animal families	6—7
Family facts	8—9
New babies	10—11
Mom's milk	12—13
Brothers and sisters	14—15
Out for the day	16—17
Home, sweet home	18—19
Rise and shine	20—21
Welcome to the world	22—23
Neat and tidy	24—25
Taking a dip	26—27
Mealtime	28—29
Eat your greens	30—31
Gone fishing	32—33
Carry me, mom	34—35
Hide and seek	36—37
Mommy and me	38—39
Playtime	40—41
Climbing trees	42—43
Using tools	44—45
Sending signals	46—47
Watch me wobble	48—49
Follow the leader	50—51
Proud parents	52—53
I need a hug	54—55
Staying safe	56—57
Time for bed	58—59
The end	60—61
Glosssary	62—63
Index	64

Wait up! Walking isn't easy with little legs. I hope we stop and rest soon.

just like us

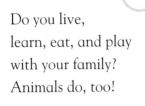

Do you live, learn, eat, and play with your family? Animals do, too!

We are animals, just like elephants, monkeys, lions, bears, and hippos are animals. Like your parents, many animal parents take care of their children and make sure they're safe.

Which of our animal families

Learning new skills and tricks is an important part of growing up.

Your mom and dad make sure you have the right foods to eat.

Animal parents often cuddle their babies, too, and play with them, and even make sure their faces and their fur are neat. About the only thing they don't do is nag about homework!

reminds you of your own?

animal families

Moms and dads together or apart, one child or lots of children, close friends or groups of relations— they're all families!

Cattle live in big groups called herds. Within one herd, many of the calves might be related. They all play, rest, and eat together.

rooster

I live with my children and their mom, and I like to make sure they all behave themselves!

hen

The people we live with are called our

More's a crowd

Do you ever go out with your friends' family? These young hippos are being looked after by two moms.

There are lots of different human families, too. Some have one parent, some have two, and some have aunts, uncles, and grandparents as well.

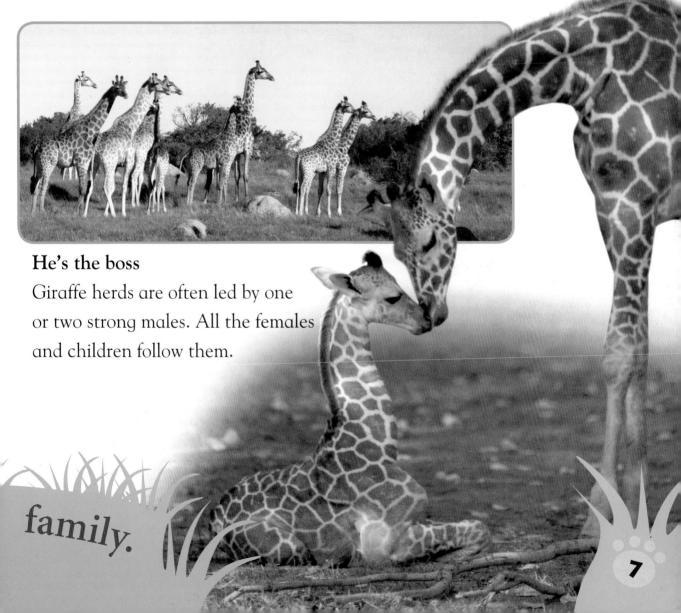

He's the boss

Giraffe herds are often led by one or two strong males. All the females and children follow them.

family.

family facts

There are all kinds of animal families with different ways of life. Here are a few:

Raccoon moms raise their children alone. They leave them in the safest place they can find, like this cozy log.

Dad's turn

If you were a seahorse dad, you would carry eggs in a safe pouch on your body until they're ready to hatch as baby seahorses.

What's life like in your family?

A male sea lion is called a bull. He has lots of wives. After mating, he will go off and live alone.

Left alone

After a baby sea lion is born (this one is *brand* new), his mom takes care of him for only a few days before she needs to go off to find food.

Turn and turn about

Baby penguins are looked after all the time. Their parents leave to find food as well, but they take turns looking after their little one.

new babies

A baby is about the most exciting thing that can arrive in a family. Newborns are very small and weak, so their moms have to take extra-special care of them.

cow and calf

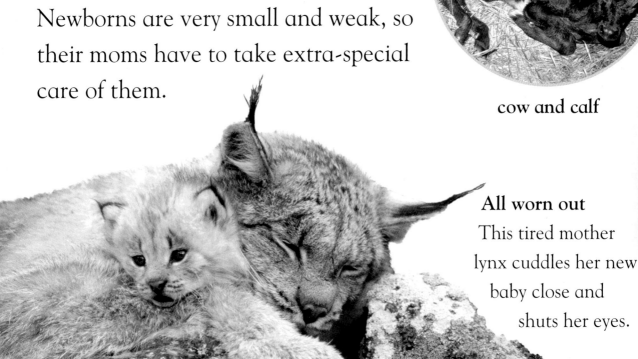

All worn out
This tired mother lynx cuddles her new baby close and shuts her eyes.

Seven or eight baby blue-tits usually hatch at one time, so their mom and dad have lots of hungry new babies to look after.

macaques

I hope he holds on really tight!

mom's milk

When they're first born, lots of baby animals live on milk they get from their mommies. Later, babies grow big enough to eat grown-up food.

orang-utans

We drink milk from our mommies, too. Some babies keep on doing this even after they've started eating real food.

Jacob sheep

Puma cubs are born blind and deaf, so it's a good thing they don't have to look far for food.

Mothers' milk is best

Liquid lunch

Babies drink milk from their mom's breasts. This hungry little sea cow (sometimes called a *manatee*) can even do it under water!

My brothers and sisters and I are all VERY hungry. Because mom sometimes has three babies, she has several breasts, or teats. I just hope there's enough milk!

grizzly bears

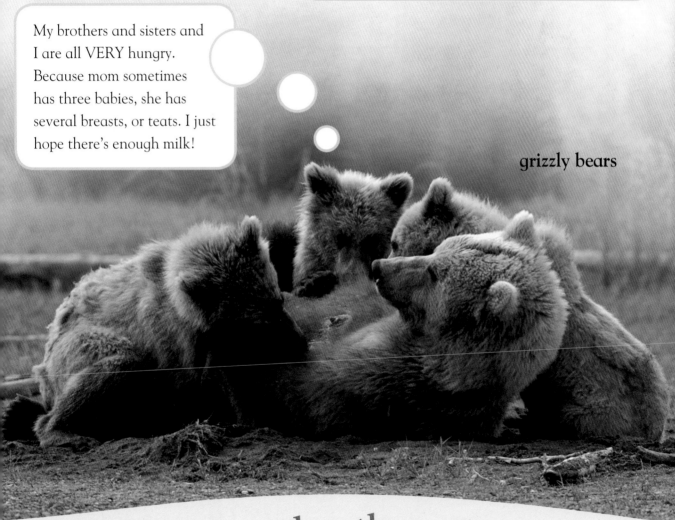

for babies—it makes them strong.

brothers and sisters

Kittens love playing with their family. Three to five are normally born together.

How many brothers and sisters do you have? Animals often have lots and lots, and sometimes they are all born at the same time!

These little piggies...

... live in a big family. Their moms usually have up to 10 babies, or even more.

Getting into mischief is so much

Sheep are a bit like people—they tend to have just one baby, or twins.

Puppy love
Big dogs like labradors can have up to 14 puppies at a time. What a lot of puppies!

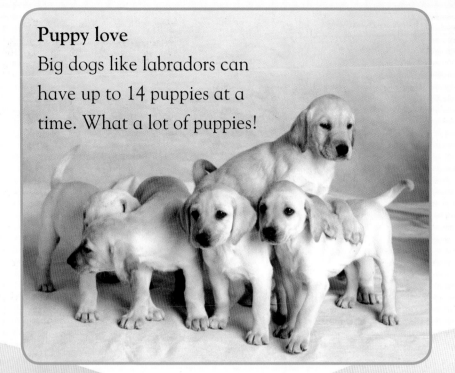

Full load
How many of her babies can this mother goosander fit on her back?

more fun when there's a gang of us.

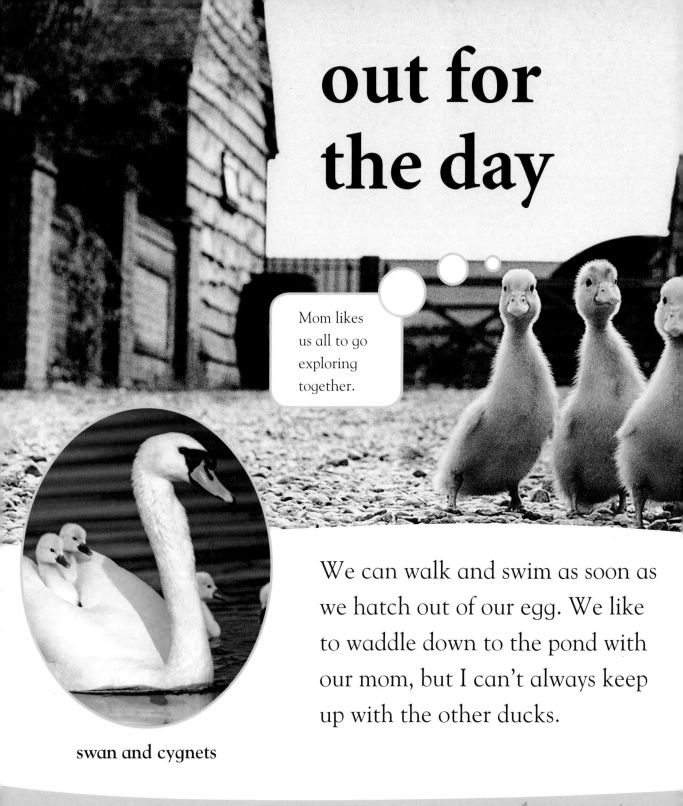

out for the day

Mom likes us all to go exploring together.

swan and cygnets

We can walk and swim as soon as we hatch out of our egg. We like to waddle down to the pond with our mom, but I can't always keep up with the other ducks.

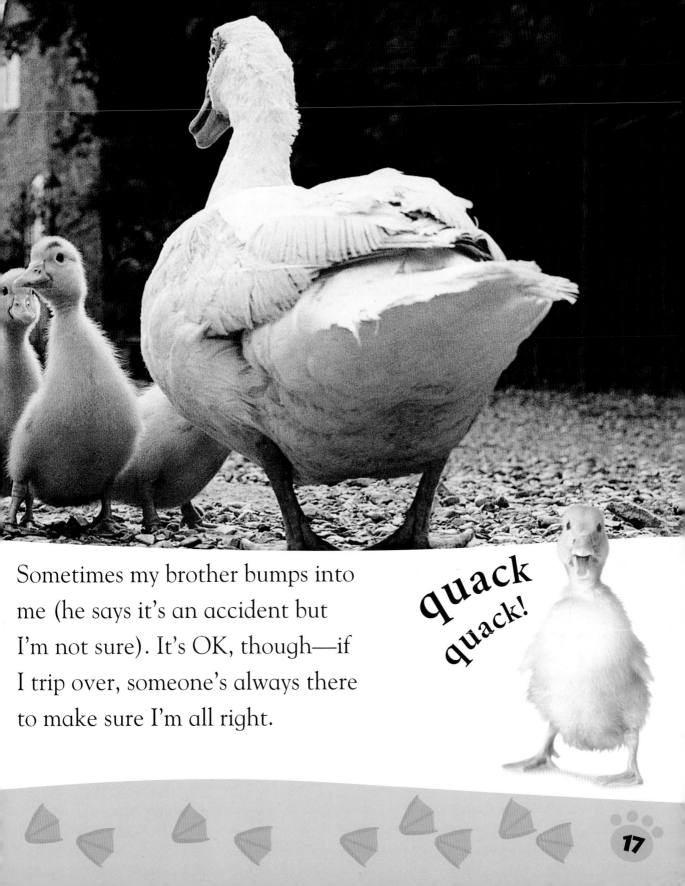

Sometimes my brother bumps into me (he says it's an accident but I'm not sure). It's OK, though—if I trip over, someone's always there to make sure I'm all right.

quack quack!

home, sweet home

tortoises

Houses keep humans safe and warm, and many animals build shelters, too. One animal—the tortoise—even carries his house around with him on his back. It's called a shell.

rabbit

After bouncing around, I like to go to sleep in my cozy underground tunnels, called a warren.

Some animals live underground—

Tree houses

Lots of birds build nests in hollow trees to keep their chicks safe. Using their beaks, the birds make soft beds out of twigs, leaves, moss, and anything else they can find.

Each night I make myself a nest from leaves and branches high in the treetops. I hope I don't fall out!

orang-utan

some live high up in the trees.

rise and shine

It's hard to get moving in the mornings when you feel warm and sleepy. Sometimes baby animals have trouble waking up, too.

Baby red foxes (called cubs) wake up in the safety of a sheltered den.

zebra

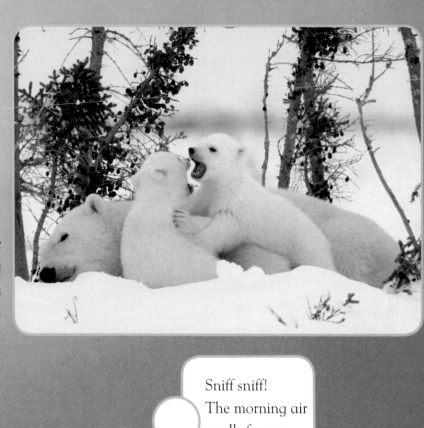

These playful polar bears are making sure their mom doesn't sleep in.

Sniff sniff! The morning air smells funny.

Even for a wild rabbit, there's nothing like a good yawn and a stretch to start the day.

gorillas

welcome to the world

Animal moms kiss and nuzzle their babies to make sure they feel close and safe. This process, which is called "bonding," continues through childhood.

cheetahs

If a new mom doesn't bond with her

Safe smell

After two or three days, a baby zebra (called a foal) knows its mom by her smell, her voice, and the way she looks. Until then, she won't let any other member of the herd near.

I get to know my mom by rubbing her furry face with my nose and licking it with my tongue.

Brrrrrr

This tiny seal has just been born on the ice in Antarctica. Its mom will soon leave to find food. When she gets back, she'll find her baby by its smell.

baby, she may not take care of it.

neat and tidy

Sometimes your mum helps you wash your face and hands and brush your hair, and sometimes you do these things yourself. Animals like to be well groomed too.

rabbit

A mother red deer licks her baby, called a fawn. This licking comforts him and keeps him neat.

Wash time
This baby lemur has both his mum and his aunt to look after him. A quick lick and his face is nice and clean.

kittens

Cats not only groom themselves, they also groom each other. If your kitten licks you, it means he likes and trusts you.

Baboons spend lots of time checking each other's fur. Tiny insects crawl in it and cause itching, so it's good to have a friend to help dig them out.

Why don't children *ever* clean their ears?

25

taking a dip

There's nothing elephants enjoy more than messing around in water holes. Once they get in, they don't ever want to get out again.

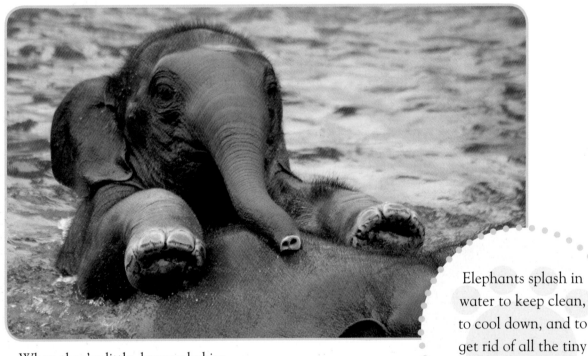

When they're little, human babies can't control their arms and legs very well. In the same way, a baby elephant's trunk is a little floppy at first.

Elephants splash in water to keep clean, to cool down, and to get rid of all the tiny bugs that live on their skin.

Baby elephants REALLY LOVE

I can suck up lots of water in my trunk, then curl it around and treat myself to a nice shower.

to play in muddy water.

mealtime

Your mom might give you meat or rice for your meals, but animal children can feed on grass, or nuts, or bugs. Birds even pop worms into their babys' beaks.

feeding chicks

Family grazing
These rhinos eat mostly grasses. Like cattle, they wander over the land, snacking as they go.

Lots of creatures, and especially big cats, eat other animals. When lion cubs play roughly together, they're learning how to hunt and kill.

If I can just get this nut open, we can have what's inside for our supper.

eat your greens

koala

Some animals, like some humans, eat only plants—no fish or meat. The trouble with eating just vegetation is that you have to eat a huge amount to give you all the energy you need.

Reach for the grub
Giraffes have *long, long* necks so they can chew the highest branches where no other animal can reach.

Seeds, nuts, and vegetables are **scrumptious!** Do you think you could be a vegetarian, too?

This forest is the perfect place to pick up a snack.

mountain gorilla

gone fishing

Yum, yum—fish for supper! Do your parents buy fish from a store and cook it for you? If young animals want fish to eat, they have to learn to catch it all by themselves.

Otters catch and eat lots and lots of fish. This mom shows her pup how it's done.

Watch and learn

Baby seals learn to catch fish when they're a few weeks old, but they can swim almost as soon as they're born. Their mom's milk puts on a thick layer of fat to keep them warm in their ice-watery home.

Fish is just as good for you as it is for baby animals—it makes your bones strong and strengthens your eyes, brain, and heart, too.

Fresh fish is very fast food—

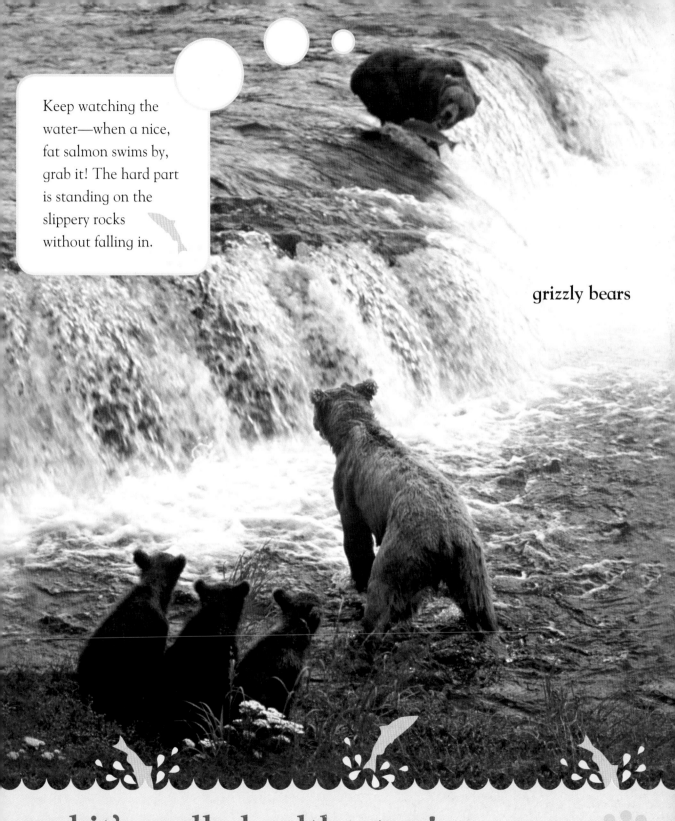

Keep watching the water—when a nice, fat salmon swims by, grab it! The hard part is standing on the slippery rocks without falling in.

grizzly bears

and it's really healthy, too!

carry me, mom

When you were very small, your mommy and daddy carried you around. Animal parents carry their babies, too— on their backs, in pouches, or even in their teeth.

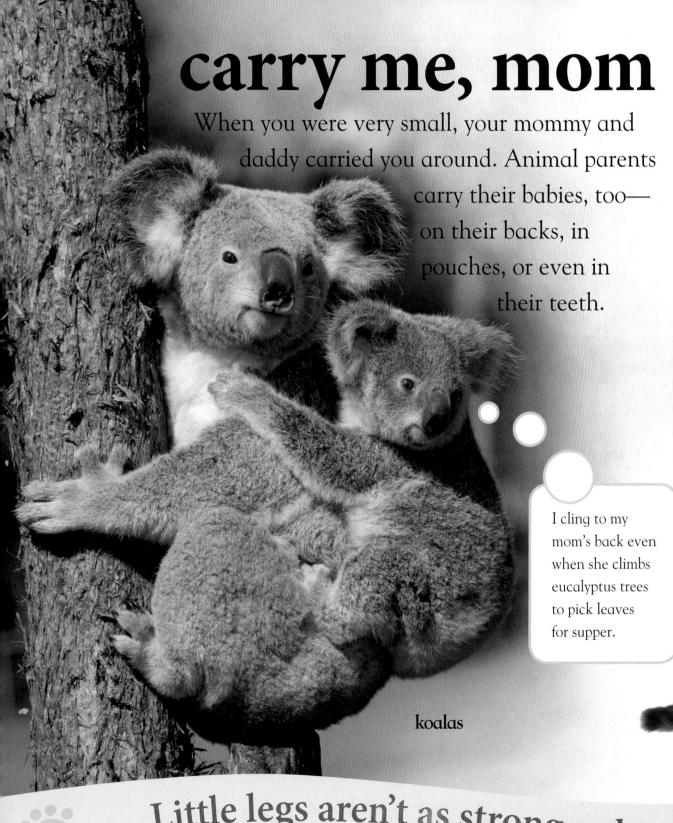

I cling to my mom's back even when she climbs eucalyptus trees to pick leaves for supper.

koalas

Little legs aren't as strong as big

A tiny wallabee stays in its mom's pouch all the time. Even older babies like to snuggle inside when they get tired of jumping.

When human children sit on grown-ups' shoulders, we say they're having a piggyback ride, but pigs don't do this!

Precious package

When they're babies, all cats—from lions to family pets—get carried in their mom's teeth. She holds the skin on their neck very very gently.

Baby gorillas can't walk far until they're about nine months old. Until then, they hang on to their mom's fur and ride on her back.

ones—sometimes they need help.

hide and seek

Certain animals are very hard to see, because they blend in with their surroundings. Sometimes their disguise protects them from enemies, and sometimes it helps them hide so they can attack other animals.

plover

plover eggs on
rocky shore

A covering that makes something

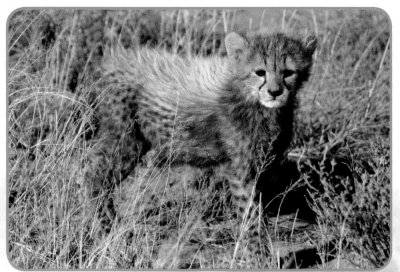

Double duty

Since his fluffy baby coat looks like grass, this young cheetah can hide from his enemies. When he grows up, he'll hide from animals he's hunting so he can pounce.

Nobody will find us here—we can nibble all this tasty grass in peace.

mountain goats

hard to see is called *camouflage.*

mommy and me

Hippopotamuses love the water—their closest living relatives are whales and porpoises. A hippo mom usually has just one baby at a time, and she keeps a very close eye on it for the first year of its life.

Hippos are so heavy, they walk along the bottom of lakes and rivers. They take their time, since adults can hold their breath for about five minutes.

Mom and I spend most of the day in the water—it keeps us cool in the hot sun. In the evening, when we get hungry, we come out to find food.

There are lots of other animals in the river and on the shore, but I always feel safe with my mom close by. She shows me where to go and protects me from danger.

playtime

What's your favorite time of day? Playtime, of course! Animal babies love to play, too—it's an important part of learning and growing up.

orang-utan

Mommy! Look at me! I can stand on my own two feet. Do I look like a big grizzly bear yet?

Play is fun! It helps you learn,

Chimpanzee trampoline

Ready or not, here I come! This chimpanzee mom plays with her baby to show her love. Do you play with your mommy?

Some play looks painful, but it's mostly for show. A good scrap helps babies learn how to hunt prey and survive in the wild.

kittens

Slip, slide, and glide

Emperor penguins never have to wish for snow! They have fun sliding on ice at the South Pole!

keep fit, and make friends.

climbing trees

Do you like climbing trees? Some animals live in trees, play in trees, and find all their food in trees, too.

brown bear

Scrambling up branches makes my muscles strong. When I grow up, I'll be too big to climb so high!

raccoons

This porcupine mom and baby climb trees to eat leaves and bark. If they eat too much, the tree will die.

Playing in trees is good exercise—

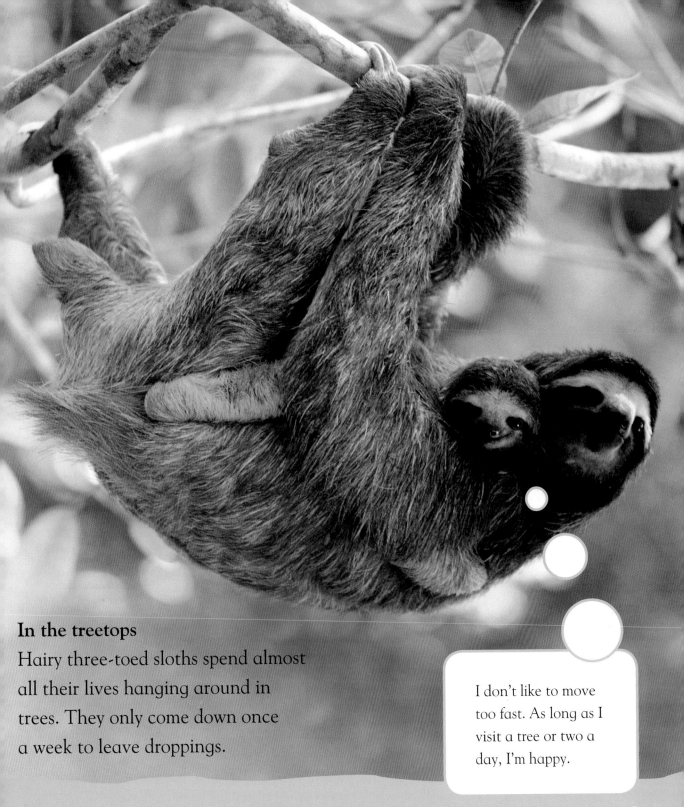

In the treetops

Hairy three-toed sloths spend almost all their lives hanging around in trees. They only come down once a week to leave droppings.

I don't like to move too fast. As long as I visit a tree or two a day, I'm happy.

as long as you don't fall out!

using tools

In the same way that you use a spoon or a fork to pick up your food, chimpanzees use sticks to collect the insects they find so delicious.

I'm sure there are lots more fat juicy ants in here.

Only the smartest animals are

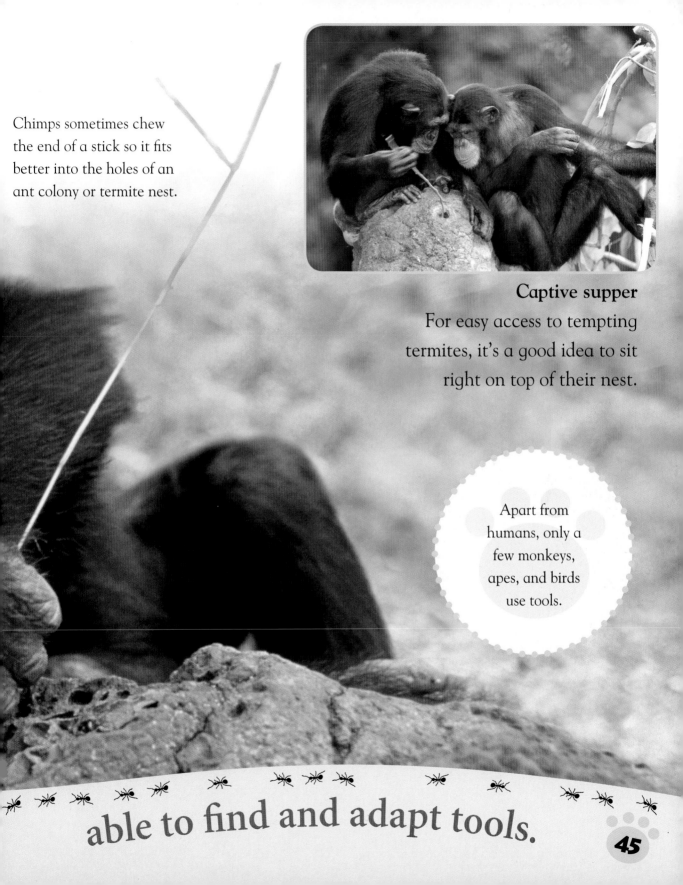

Chimps sometimes chew the end of a stick so it fits better into the holes of an ant colony or termite nest.

Captive supper
For easy access to tempting termites, it's a good idea to sit right on top of their nest.

Apart from humans, only a few monkeys, apes, and birds use tools.

able to find and adapt tools.

sending signals

Mommy, where are you? Babies and parents talk to each other in many ways. A lost penguin chick recognizes its mother's voice from thousands of others. But baby-talk isn't just about sound...

penguin

Barking orders
Seal moms grunt and touch to show love and protect their newborn babies.

Parents use signals to comfort,

bottle-nose dolphin

Clickety-click. Listen to my songs and clicks and follow along.

meerkats

Look out
Playtime is safe with meerkat dad keeping watch. His children can tell just by the way he stands and looks that he's watching over them.

protect, and teach their babies.

watch me wobble

Almost all grass-eating animals—like horses and zebras—have to stand up on their feet in the first hour after they're born. No wonder they're a little wobbly!

It's hard to keep your balance when your legs are so long and thin!

Baby wildebeests need a lot of get up and go—their herds are always on the move, so they have to run about 20 minutes after they're born.

follow the leader

When groups of animals move from place to place, one adult usually leads the way. Babies and children follow along behind...

Baby polar bears stay with mom when she goes off to find food. This outing is probably their first—and their mom's first—since they were born.

penguin chicks

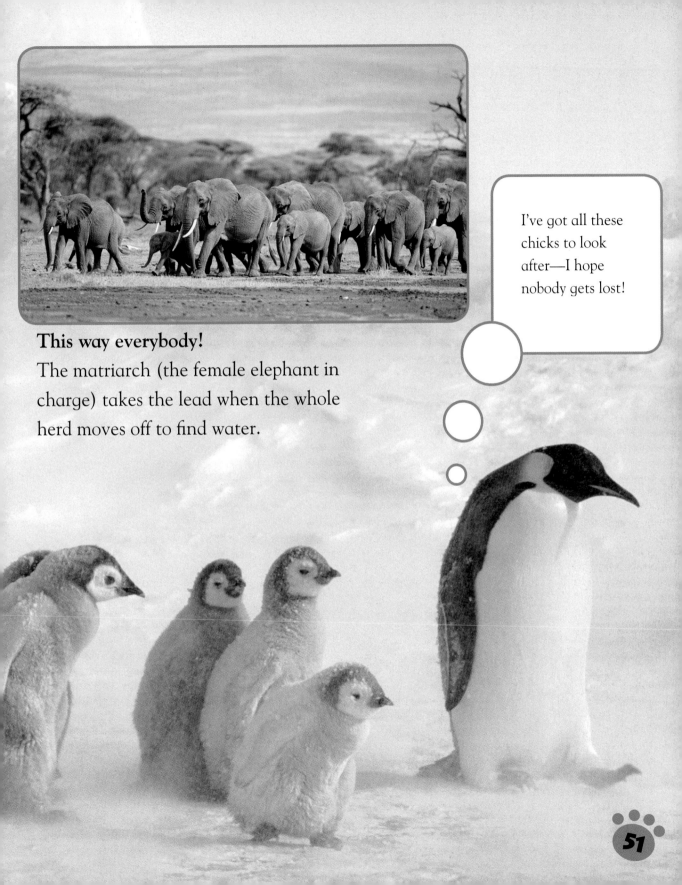

This way everybody!
The matriarch (the female elephant in charge) takes the lead when the whole herd moves off to find water.

I've got all these chicks to look after—I hope nobody gets lost!

proud parents

lion cub

Lions are the rulers of the jungle—fierce hunters that all the other animals are afraid of. When it comes to their children, though, mommy and daddy lions are big pussycats.

Hello mom

When it's bonding with its mother, a baby lion crawls all over her and enjoys a little friendly pushing and shoving, too.

Sometimes human babies hurt their parents when they don't mean to, by scratching, or biting, or poking.

Loving parents often allow

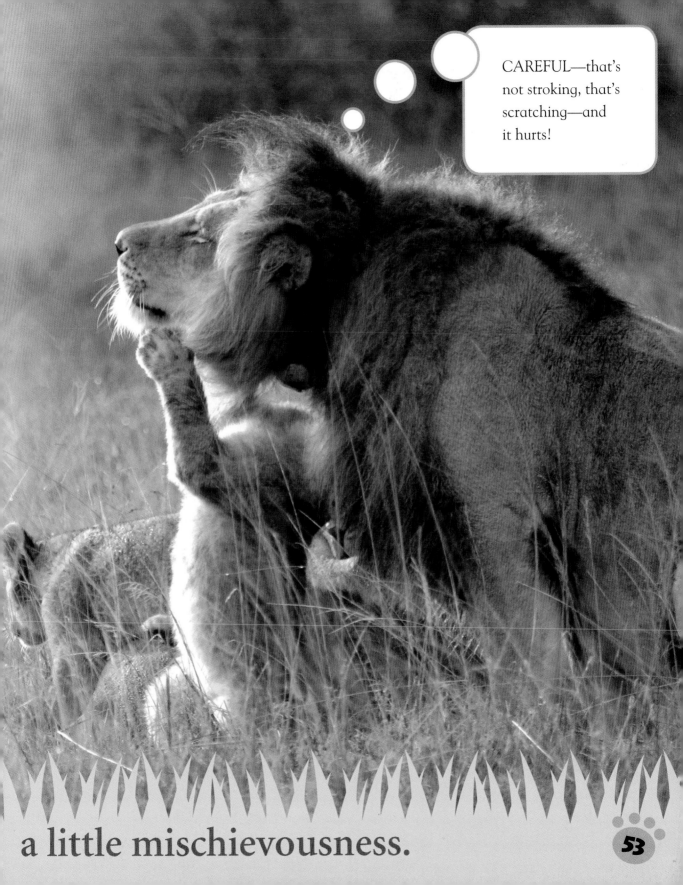

a little mischievousness.

I need a hug

When you're tired, or sad, or frightened, a hug is the very nicest thing. Animals comfort their families, too—in whatever way suits them best.

These ring-tailed lemurs all want a hug from mom at the same time.

There, there
Elephants can't hug each other like we can, but an older sister's reassuring trunk has the same effect.

A comforting cuddle always

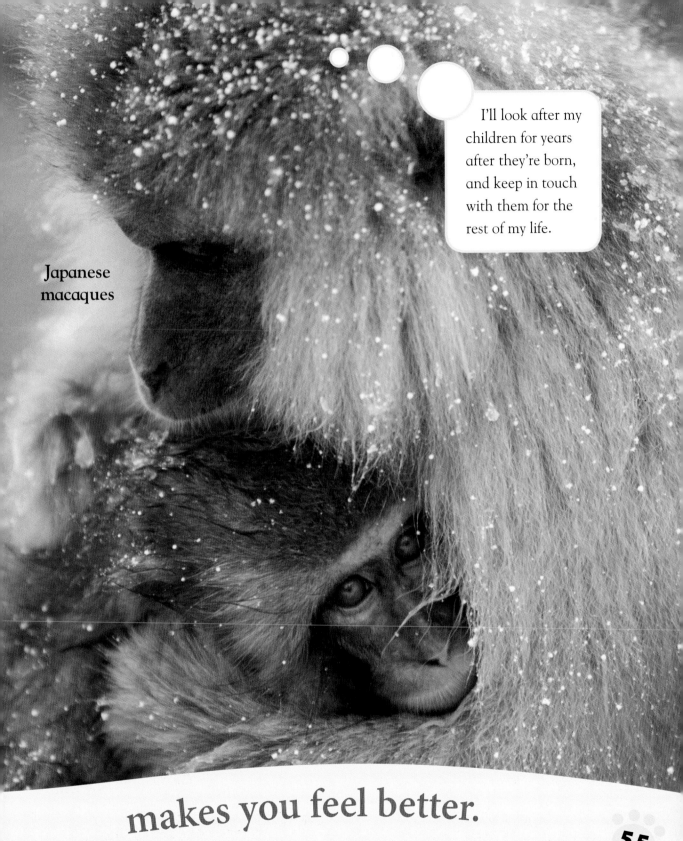

Japanese
macaques

I'll look after my children for years after they're born, and keep in touch with them for the rest of my life.

makes you feel better.

staying safe

All through the animal kingdom, mothers and fathers do everything they can to keep their children safe. Their protection can take many different forms.

Eyes focused

Meerkat families search for food in the warm sunshine. Here, the little ones scour the ground in search of insects, while the grown-ups keep a protective watch.

polar bears

When I feel scared, I try to hide behind my mom's big, furry body.

If there is danger, shaggy muskoxen make a circle around their young. These parents are just moving into place.

dormouse

time for bed

Some baby animals sleep at night, some during the day. Some sleep in nests, some in trees—and some just find a nice patch of ground.

We like to sleep during the day, when the sun is hot. During the cool night, we look for food.

Zzzzzzzzzzzzzzzzzzz

In the treetops

Squirrel monkeys not only spend all day in the trees, they sleep there, too. They have a special instinct, or sense, that stops them from falling off.

Animals that are active during the day and sleep at night (like you and me) are called *diurnal.* The ones that sleep during the day are called *nocturnal.*

Baby owls (called owlets) sleep in trees, too. These brothers and sisters snuggle together on a safe branch.

ZZZZZZZZZZZZZZZZZZzzzzzzzzzzz...............

the end

Now you've seen how lots of animals live with their families. Which baby animal did you like best?

gorilla

Please come and

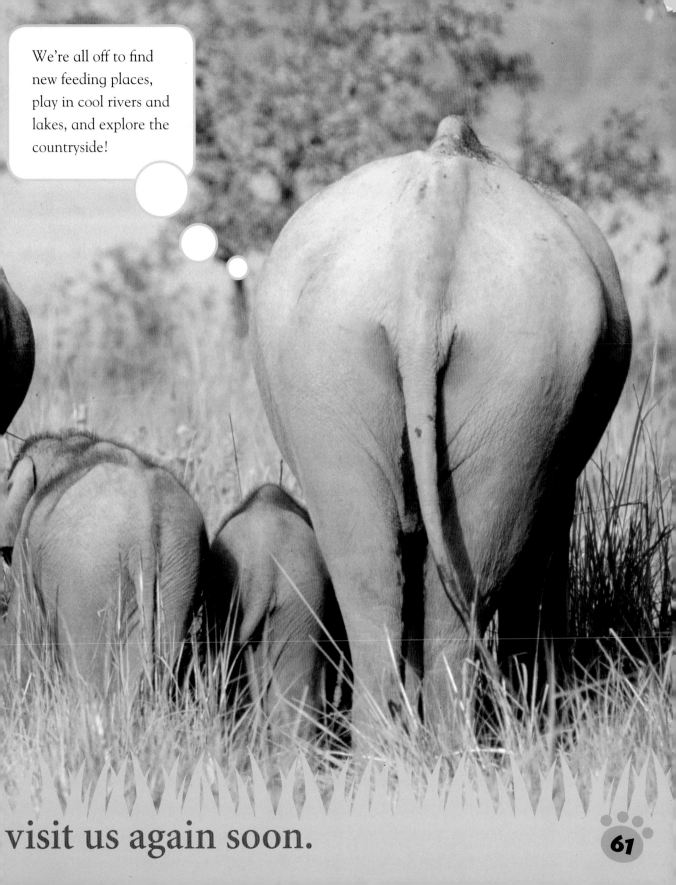

We're all off to find new feeding places, play in cool rivers and lakes, and explore the countryside!

visit us again soon.

glossary

What does it all mean? Here are the meanings of some words that will help you learn about animal families.

bonding when a parent and baby take time to know and love each other.

breasts the area of an animal that produces milk.

brood a collection of young animals cared for at one time.

colony a group of animals (like penguins) that live closely together.

diurnal an animal that is awake during the day and sleeps at night.

herd a large group of animals that travels together.

instinct natural feeling animals have from birth (rather than something they learn), which helps them survive.

mammal an animal with fur that drinks its mother's milk when it's a baby.

mating when a male and female come together to produce babies.

matriarch the female in charge of a group of animals.

nocturnal an animal that is awake at night and sleeps during the day.

prey an animal that is hunted for food.

relatives members of a family, like brothers and sisters, uncles and aunts.

teat the nipple of a female where a baby drinks milk.

The bigger you grow, the

picture credits

The publisher would like to thank the following for their kind permission to reproduce their photographs:

(Key: a-above; b-below/bottom; c-center; l-left; r-right; t-top): **Alamy Images:** Arco Images 14tl; Steve Austin/ Papilio 9bl; Blickwinkel/ Kaufung 24cl; Blickwinkel/ Weber 6tr; Andrew Fox 29bc, bl, br; Jonathan Hewitt 26c; Juniors Bildarchiv 6b; Erich Kuchling/ Westend 61 15c; Thomas D Mangelsen/ Peter Arnold, Inc. 33; Martin Phelps 14c; Photo Network/ Bill Bachmann 4bl; Steve Bloom Images 7tc, 28bc, br; Duncan Usher 21br, 24tl; Brent Ward 7br; WorldFoto 46tr. **Ardea:** Uno Berggren 19tr; Elizabeth Bomford 32cl; John Daniels 54tl; Jagdeep Rajput 60-61. **Corbis:** O. Alamany & E. Vicens 11t; Tom Brakefield 55; W. Perry Conway 10c; George McCarthy 11br; Joe McDonald 28cr; Paul Souders 22tl, 27; Gabriela Staebler/ Zefa 23tr; Kennan Ward 57br. **DK Images:** Barleylands Farm Museum and Animal Centre, Billericay 15cla; Two Hand Promotions 7cl, 22-23, 30crb, 37tl, 38bc, br, 39bc, bl, br, 52c, 53, 56c, 59t. **Michael Fiddleman 2008:** 9tl. **FLPA:** Tui De Roy/ Minden Pictures 18tl; Tim Fitzharris/ Minden Pictures 42cr; Michael & Patricia Fogden/ Minden Pictures 43; Sumio Harada/ Minden Pictures 37b; Mitsuaki Iwago/ Minden Pictures 34; Frans Lanting 1, 32cr; Yva Momatiuk & John Eastcott/ Minden Pictures 40b; Pete Oxford/ Minden Pictures 29t; Fritz Polking 31; Ingo Schulz/ Imagebroker 35tl; Jurgen & Christine Sohns 46c; Sunset 41cr; Tom Vezo/ Minden Pictures 36cla; Michael Weber/ Imagebroker 47; Konrad Wothe/ Minden Pictures 36b, 42br, cl; Norbert Wu/ Minden Pictures 23cr. **Getty Images:** James Balog 44-45; The Image Bank/ Andy Rouse 52tl; The Image Bank/ Daniel J. Cox 8cr; The Image Bank/ Joseph Van Os 50-51; Beverly Joubert/ National Geographic 38-39c; Jochen Luebke/ AFP 38cl; Michael Melford 54b; Minden Pictures/ Norbert Wu 8bl; Minden Pictures/ ZSSD 60tl; Photographer's Choice/ Daniel J Cox 20cra; Photographer's Choice/ Johan Elzenga 5br; Photographer's Choice RR/ Ronald Wittek 8tl; Reportage/ Paula Bronstein 2; Riser/ Darrell Gulin 25; Robert Harding World Imagery/ Thorsten Milse 21tr, 50cra; Science Faction/ Konrad Wothe 9tr; Manoj Shah 45tr; Stone - Daniel J Cox 56-57; Stone/ Anup Shah 58c; Stone/ David Trood 4-5t; Stone/ Jose Luis Pelaez 5cr; Taxi/ Benelux Press 28tl; Taxi/ Stan Osolinski 51tl. **iStockphoto.com:** Debra McGuire 47. **naturepl.com:** Eric Baccega 3, 13b; Bernard Castelein 59cr; Todd Pusser 13tr; Gabriel Rojo 12cr; Anup Shah 12tl, 40tl, 41tr, 48bc, br, cl, 49bc, bl, br; Shattil & Rozinski 63; Carol Walker 48-49; Wegner/ Arco 35cr. **NHPA/ Photoshot:** Stephen Dalton 58tl. **Photolibrary:** OSF/ Rob Nunnington 20-21; OSF/ Mike Powles 24cr. **PunchStock:** Digital Vision 10tr, 16-17; Photodisc/ John Giustina 5tr. **Still Pictures:** Compost/ Visage 19b. **SuperStock:** Age Fotostock 16clb; ZSSD 30tl.

Jacket images: Front: **Getty Images:** Robert Harding World Imagery/ Thorsten Milse. Back: **Alamy Images:** Steve Bloom Images c; **Corbis:** Paul Souders cl.

All other images © Dorling Kindersley
For further information see: www.dkimages.com

deer

Learning is fun, but some things are hard. My mom helps me learn and understand.

bigger the words you know.

index

ants 44–45

baboons 25
bathing 26–27
bears 4, 13, 33, 40, 42
blue-tits 10–11, 19

cats 14, 24, 35, 41
cattle 6
cheetah 22, 37
chimpanzees 41, 44–45
climbing 19, 34, 42–43, 59
cows 10

deer 24
dogs 15
dolphins 47
dormouse 58
ducks 16–17

elephants 4, 26-27, 51,
   54, 60–61

feeding 12–13, 28–29, 30–31,
   32–33, 37, 38, 42, 44–45

fish 32–33
foxes 20

giraffe 7, 30, 48–49
goats 37
gorillas 22, 31, 35, 60
grooming 24–25

hen 6
hippopotamus 4, 7, 38–39
horses 48
hunting 28–29, 32–33, 37, 41

koalas 30, 34

lemurs 24, 54
lions 4, 28–29, 52–53, 58
lynx 10

macaques 11, 55
meerkats 47, 56
monkeys 4, 29, 59
muskoxen 57

orangutan 12, 19, 40
otters 32
owls 59

penguins 9, 41, 46, 50–51
pigs 14
playing 28, 40–41, 47
plover 36
polar bears 21, 50, 57

porcupine 42
porpoises 38
puma 12

rabbits 18, 21, 24
raccoons 8, 42
rhinoceros 28
rooster 6

sea cows 13
seahorses 8
sea lions 9
seals 23, 32, 46
sheep 12, 15
sleeping 18, 58–59
sloth 43
swans 16

termites 45
tortoises 18

wallaby 35
whales 38
wildebeests 48–49

zebras 20–21, 23, 48

DK would like to thank Rob Nunn, Julia Harris-Voss, Natalie Godwin, and Two Hands Productions Ltd. for help with this book.